SCIENCE EXPLORER

WITHDRAWN

SOLAR ENERGY

SUPER COOL
SCIENCE
EXPERIMENTS:
SOLAR ENERGY

by Christine Taylor-Butler

CHERRY LAKE PUBLISHING • ANN ARBOR, MICHIGAN

CHERRY
LAKE
Publishing

Published in the United States of America by
Cherry Lake Publishing
Ann Arbor, Michigan
www.cherrylakepublishing.com

Content Editor: Robert Wolffe, EdD,
Professor of Teacher Education,
Bradley University, Peoria, Illinois

Book design and illustration: The Design Lab

Photo Credits: Cover and page 1, ©PHOTOCREO Michal Bednarek, used under license from Shutterstock, Inc.; page 7, ©iStock.com/pastorscott; page 11, ©iStock.com/nycshooter; page 12, ©iStock.com/IDFK303; page 16, ©iStock.com/Yakobchuk; page 17, ©iStock.com/edfuentesg; page 21, ©iStock.com/7rendered; page 25, ©iStock.com/Woldee

Library of Congress Cataloging-in-Publication Data
Taylor-Butler, Christine.
  Super cool science experiments: Solar energy /
by Christine Taylor-Butler.
      p. cm.—(Science explorer)
  Includes bibliographical references and index.
  ISBN-13: 978-1-60279-527-3   ISBN-10: 1-60279-527-4 (lib. bdg.)
  ISBN-13: 978-1-60279-606-5   ISBN-10: 1-60279-606-8 (pbk.)
  1. Solar energy—Juvenile literature. I. Title. II. Title: Solar energy.
III. Series.
  TJ810.3.T39 2010
  621.47078—dc22   2009006837

Cherry Lake Publishing would like to acknowledge the work of The Partnership for 21st Century Skills. Please visit www.21stcenturyskills.org for more information.

SCIENCE EXPLORER

SOLAR ENERGY

TABLE OF CONTENTS

4 Soak Up Some Sun!

5 First Things First

8 Experiment #1: Up, Up, and Away!

12 Experiment #2: What Color Is the Sun?

17 Experiment #3: Clean Water from Solar Power

21 Experiment #4: How Does Your Garden Grow?

25 Experiment #5: Hot Dog!

29 Experiment #6: Do It Yourself!

30 Glossary

31 For More Information

32 Index

32 About the Author

Soak Up Some Sun!

Let's come up with some bright ideas about solar energy!

It's big. It's blazing. What is it? The sun! The sun is nature's giant lightbulb. Have you ever stopped to really think about the sun, or about how the sun's energy affects something and can make it change forms?

You probably already know that science is fun. But did you know that you can do experiments with things you already have at home? If you've ever wondered about the sun and its energy—and wanted to find out more—you are already one step closer to thinking like a scientist. In this book, we'll learn how scientists think. We'll do that by experimenting with solar energy, or energy from the sun. We'll even learn how to design our own experiments. It's time to make some bright discoveries!

First Things First

Scientists learn by studying something very carefully. For example, some scientists who study the sun run experiments to see how light and heat affect Earth. They notice how sunlight is turned into energy that can be used by plants. Other scientists do experiments to see if the sun's energy can replace the fuels we use.

Good scientists take notes on everything they discover. They write down their observations. Sometimes those observations lead scientists to ask new questions. With new questions in mind, they design experiments to find the answers.

When scientists design experiments, they must think very clearly. The way they think about problems is

Scientists write down what they observe.

5

often called the scientific method. What is the scientific method? It's a step-by-step way of finding answers to specific questions. The steps don't always follow the same pattern. Sometimes scientists change their minds. The process often works something like this:

Scientific method →

- **Step One:** A scientist gathers the facts and makes observations about one particular thing.
- **Step Two:** The scientist comes up with a question that is not answered by all the observations and facts.
- **Step Three:** The scientist creates a hypothesis. This is a statement of what the scientist thinks is probably the answer to the question.
- **Step Four:** The scientist tests the hypothesis. He or she designs an experiment to see whether the hypothesis is correct. The scientist does the experiment and writes down what happens.
- **Step Five:** The scientist draws a conclusion based on how the experiment turned out. The conclusion might be that the hypothesis is correct. Sometimes, though, the hypothesis is not correct. In that case, the scientist might develop a new hypothesis and another experiment.

In the following experiments, we'll see the scientific method in action. We'll gather some facts and observations about solar energy. And for each experiment, we'll develop a question and a hypothesis. Next, we'll do an actual experiment to see if our hypothesis is correct. By the end of the experiment, we should know something new about solar energy. Scientists, are you ready? Then let's get started!

Get ready to learn about the sun!

Experiment #1
Up, Up, and Away!

Playing sports in the sun can heat you up!

First, let's gather some observations. What do you already know about solar energy? You probably know that the sun provides light in the daytime. The sun also provides heat that warms Earth. Scientists know that light is a form of energy that can change into heat, another form of energy. They also know that different colors absorb different amounts of light. Have you ever worn a dark outfit on a sunny day? Did you feel very warm?

This leads to another question. Why do some colors make us feel hotter in sunlight than others? Could some colors absorb more light than others? Think about it. Here is a possible hypothesis for our first experiment: **Darker colors absorb more sunlight than lighter colors.** Now you can set up an experiment to test the hypothesis.

Here's what you'll need:
- 2 paintbrushes
- 2 clear plastic bottles
- 1 container of black paint
- 1 container of white paint
- 1 black balloon
- 1 white balloon
- a sunny window

You can get paint at a hardware store or a craft store.

Instructions:

1. Use a paintbrush to completely paint one bottle black.
2. Paint the other bottle white using the second paintbrush.
3. Set the bottles aside to dry.
4. After the paint has dried, attach the opening of the black balloon to the neck of the black bottle.
5. Attach the white balloon to the neck of the white bottle.
6. Set the bottles on a sunny windowsill. Wait 10 minutes. Observe what happens to the balloons.

Did your balloons look like this?

Conclusion:

What happened to the balloons after the bottles sat in the sun? Did they inflate? Did both fill with air? Which balloon started to inflate first?

Dark colors absorb more light than they actually reflect. The opposite is true of light colors. Sunlight is made up of different colors of light. When an object absorbs all of the colors of light, our eyes see the color black. When all of the colors of light are reflected, or bounced back, from an object, it looks white. Remember that light can be changed into heat. The darker bottle absorbed more solar energy than the lighter one. That energy heated the air inside the bottle. The heated air expanded and inflated the balloon. Does this explain your results? Was your hypothesis correct?

Run another trial of this experiment. This time, attach a black balloon to a clear bottle. Attach a white balloon to another clear bottle. Put the unpainted bottles on a sunny windowsill for 10 minutes. What happens? Compare these results to your findings with the painted bottles. Which balloon showed the biggest change?

Solar energy heats some parts of Earth more than others. So the air above some places becomes warmer than others. Hot air rises because it is less dense and therefore lighter than cool air. Warmer air has more energy and spreads out. Cooler air sinks. Have you ever seen a hot air balloon? Air inside the balloon is heated using a gas burner. The heated air causes the balloon to rise. How does the balloon return to the ground? The balloon starts to sink after the air inside is no longer heated with the burner and it begins to cool. The pilot may also open a valve in the top of the balloon to let some of the hot air escape.

Experiment #2
What Color Is the Sun?

Which car will absorb the most solar energy?

We learned from Experiment #1 that solar energy heats dark colors more than light colors. This explains why black seats in a car feel very hot in the summer, but beige seats do not. Let's take our findings from the last experiment a step farther. What about specific colors? Do different colors absorb sunlight at different rates? Here is a new hypothesis: **Color can change the amount of heat that is absorbed by an object.**

Here's what you'll need:

- 7 clear plastic cups that are the same size
- A ruler
- Scissors
- 6 sheets of colored construction paper: one each of black, white, red, blue, green, and yellow
- Tape
- 7 ice cubes that are the same size
- A timer
- A piece of paper and a pencil
- a sunny window

You'll want to keep the ice in the freezer until you are ready for it.

Make sure your paper strips are long enough to wrap around the cups.

Instructions:

1. Measure the height of your cups with a ruler.
2. Cut a strip from each sheet of colored paper that is the same height as the cups. The strips should also be long enough to completely wrap around the cups.
3. Use tape to secure 1 strip of colored paper around each cup. Use a different color for each cup. One cup will be left uncovered.
4. Cut a 4-inch (10.2 centimeter) square from each color of leftover construction paper. Cut larger squares if these don't completely cover the top of each cup.

5. Place 1 ice cube in each cup. Then place each square on top of the cup that is wrapped with the same color of paper. The clear cup of ice will not be covered with paper.
6. Place the cups near a sunny window. Wait 1 minute. Use the timer to keep track of the time. After 1 minute, peek inside each cup. Have the ice cubes started to melt? If so, how much of each ice cube has melted? You can use your ruler to measure the height of the water. Record your observations on a sheet of paper.
7. Check the progress once each minute for 15 minutes. Record how much water has melted each time. How many minutes does it take each sample to completely melt?

Conclusion:
Which ice cube melted the fastest? Which cup was it in? Which ice cube melted slowest? What color was the cup it was in? How did the results of the colored cups compare to the cup that was not covered in paper? Do different colors absorb solar energy at different rates? Remember that light energy can be changed into heat energy when absorbed by a color. This heat is what helps melt the ice. If the ice melted at different rates, does that mean the cups produced different amounts of heat? Was your hypothesis correct?

Can you see ROY G. BIV in this picture?

Sunlight is made up of many light waves. Each wave contains a different amount of energy. When sunlight hits water droplets in the sky, the light bends at different angles. This light separates into different colors before being reflected out of the drops. The bands of color are red, orange, yellow, green, blue, indigo, and violet. The result of this process is a rainbow. A good way to remember the colors of a rainbow is to use the first letter of each color to make a name: Roy G. Biv.

Experiment #3

Clean Water from Solar Power

How long do you think it would take solar energy to evaporate this water?

In Experiment #2, solar energy heated the ice cubes and turned them into a liquid. If the sun's energy heated the water long enough, it would disappear into the air as vapor. This process is called evaporation.

You have probably noticed a muddy puddle on the ground. Have you ever paid attention to raindrops that fall from the sky? Do the drops look clear or dirty? What's going on here? Could the water in those clean drops have started out as dirty water on Earth? Do solar energy and evaporation play a role in this process? Come up with a hypothesis. Here is a possible one: **Solar energy can make dirty water clean.**

Here's what you'll need:
- Salt, coarse black pepper, sugar, and other spices
- 1 tablespoon of soil
- Spoon
- Large glass filled with water
- Coffee cup
- Clear mixing bowl
- Plastic food wrap
- Rubber bands
- Small rock

You can find most of these items in your kitchen.

SALT

Oregano

Basil

PEPPER

CHILI POWDER

PLASTIC WRAP

Your bowl will end up looking like this.

Instructions:

1. Mix the salt, pepper, sugar, spices, and soil into the water in the glass. Stir until it is no longer clear.
2. Place the coffee cup in the center of the mixing bowl.
3. Pour the dirty water into the bowl until it reaches just below the rim of the cup. Do not get water inside the cup.
4. Cover the bowl with plastic wrap. Do not stretch it tight. It should give a little. Poke the plastic wrap with your finger in the area above the empty cup to make a dip. Use rubber bands to hold the plastic wrap against the sides of the bowl.
5. Place the rock in the dip of the plastic wrap as a weight. The plastic wrap should dip down toward the cup, but not touch it.
6. Set the bowl next to a sunny window. Wait 1 hour. What is happening inside the bowl? Check the bowl again in 24 hours. Has something changed? Record your observations.

Conclusion:

What do you see on the underside of the plastic wrap? Are there droplets? What do you see in the cup? Is there any water inside?

Solar energy heated the water molecules. Some of the water evaporated and became a vapor. When this vapor hit the plastic, it cooled and turned back into a liquid. This process is called condensation. The spices and soil are solids and cannot turn into vapor at these temperatures. They remained in the bowl. The water that dripped into the cup was clean. Was your hypothesis correct?

Rain is made when solar energy heats water on Earth. When water evaporates, the vapor rises into the air. Droplets form as the water vapor cools and comes into contact with bits of dust in the air. Many droplets help make up clouds. Eventually, the drops in clouds become too heavy. The liquid falls back to Earth as rain or snow or in some other form. This entire process is called the water cycle. Solar energy is the main source of fuel for this cycle.

Experiment #4

How Does Your Garden Grow?

↰ plants need energy from the sun.

The sun's energy affects everything on Earth. We know, for instance, that farmers plant crops in places with sunlight. This might lead you to another question. What happens to some forms of life if there is no sunlight? Think about green plants and sunlight as you come up with a hypothesis. A possible hypothesis is: **Green plants need sunlight to stay healthy.**

Here's what you'll need:
- 2 glass jars that are the same size
- Small pebbles
- Potting soil
- 2 small green plants that are the same kind and size (bean plants work well)
- Water
- Sunny window
- Dark closet

Do you have everything you need?

22

Instructions:

1. Fill each jar with a 1-inch (2.5 cm) layer of pebbles.

2. Pour 2 inches (5.1 cm) of soil on top of the pebbles in each jar.

3. Make a small hole in the soil for the roots, and place one plant in each jar. Add water to each jar until the soil is moist. Make sure the soil stays moist throughout the experiment.

4. Place one jar near a sunny window. Place the other jar in a warm, dark closet.

5. Look at each jar every day for 10 days. Observe the plants. How do they look? Study the plants at the same time of day each day.

Write down what you observe each day.

Conclusion:

How have the plants changed over the course of this experiment? Does the plant in the dark look very different from the one in the light? Does it seem healthy? How can you tell? What color are its leaves? Are they pale or yellow?

Green plants are amazing. They can make their own food and give off oxygen in a process called photosynthesis. They use water and carbon dioxide to produce sugar. Where does the energy to do this come from? Sunlight, or solar energy! Some types of plants like to grow in shady areas. But green plants contain a special green substance that helps them use the sun's energy. Without light, the plants cannot make this substance. The leaves become pale. Does this explain your findings? What might happen if you took the plant out of the darkness and put it in sunlight? Was your hypothesis correct?

Have you ever seen a field of sunflowers? As they grow, the flower buds face the sun no matter where it is in the sky. When sunlight hits the sunflower, the shaded side of the stem grows faster than the side in the light. This causes the flower bud to bend toward the light. As the sun rises in the east, the sunflowers will turn east. As the sun sets in the west, the sunflowers will face west! Once a sunflower blooms, it stops moving and faces east all day.

Experiment #5

Hot Dog!

← How much heat does it take to fry an egg?

You may have heard the saying, "It's so hot you can fry an egg outside!" But is this really possible? You know that sunlight can sometimes make an object too hot to touch. You also learned that black absorbs the sun's energy faster than other colors. Do you think solar energy can cook something? Think of a hypothesis. Here are two options you might want to test. Choose the one you think is correct:

Hypothesis #1: Sunlight contains enough energy to cook food.

Hypothesis #2: Sunlight does not contain enough energy to cook food.

Here's what you'll need:

- 1 clean, empty pizza box
- Marker
- Ruler
- Scissors
- Aluminum foil
- Glue
- Clear plastic wrap
- Masking tape
- Black construction paper
- Hot dog
- Outdoor thermometer
- Oven or baking thermometer

Instructions:

1. Draw a square on the top of the pizza box using a marker. The edges of the pizza box should be 2 inches (5.1 cm) from each side of the square.
2. Carefully cut along the sides and front of the square with the scissors to make a flap. Do not cut along the line that is closest to the back of the box. This will be the hinge of the flap you just created. Carefully lift the flap until it is vertical.
3. Cut a piece of aluminum foil that is large enough to cover the side of the flap that faces the inside of the pizza box. Make sure the shinier side of the foil is facing toward you. Glue it in place.
4. Cover the hole in your box top with plastic wrap. Make sure it is stretched tight to prevent air

from leaking. Tape the edges of the plastic wrap down on the underside of the pizza box top.

5. Open the pizza box. Cut a piece of aluminum foil large enough to cover the bottom and inner sides of the pizza box. Smooth any wrinkles, and then glue the foil to the inside of the box, shiny side up. Place the sheet of black construction paper on top of the foil that is on the base of the pizza box. You've made a solar oven!

6. Place a hot dog in the middle of your oven. Set your oven outside in a hot, sunny spot.

7. Measure the outside temperature with the outdoor thermometer, and write it on a piece of paper. Place the oven thermometer inside your box.

8. Close the pizza box. Open the flap so that the sun's rays hit the foil on the flap and shine through the plastic into the bottom of your box. It may take some time to get this set up just right. Use tape to keep the flap in the correct position, if necessary.

You've built a solar oven!

Conclusion:

Check the thermometer after several minutes. How hot did it get inside the solar oven? Were you able to cook the hot dog? If so, how long did it take? The foil on the flap reflected and concentrated the sunlight through the plastic and into the pizza box. The black paper helped absorb this sunlight. The plastic helped prevent the heat from escaping. Was your hypothesis correct?

Is your hot dog hot?

The sun is more than 92 million miles (148 million km) away. But its light and energy can reach Earth in 8 minutes. Only a tiny amount of the sun's energy reaches Earth. Even so, more solar energy reaches the United States in one day than all the other sources of fuel used by humans in a year. The sun is a great source of renewable energy. Many people use solar collectors and solar cells to heat and power buildings. Solar cells are objects that turn sunlight into electricity. Your pizza box oven is a type of solar collector.

Experiment #6
Do It Yourself!

Wasn't making a solar oven to cook food exciting? But don't stop there. Come up with another experiment using a solar oven. What would happen if you changed the color of the construction paper inside the oven? Or replaced the shiny foil with white paper? Would that affect your results? What if you tried to use the oven during different times of the day? Is it possible to cook an egg or melt a marshmallow with your solar oven?

These are all great questions. Come up with a hypothesis. Then design and run an experiment. Record your observations and state your conclusion. Now that you can think like a scientist, you can see that solar energy really is hot stuff!

Okay, scientists! Now you know many new things about solar energy. Experts believe that the sun will provide light and heat for another 6 billion years. That gives you plenty of time to try out new experiments!

GLOSSARY

absorb (ab-ZORB) to soak up

conclusion (kuhn-KLOO-zhuhn) a final decision, thought, or opinion

condensation (kahn-den-SAY-shuhn) the process in which a gas changes to a liquid or solid

evaporation (i-vah-puh-RAY-shuhn) the process in which a liquid changes to a gas or vapor

hypothesis (hy-POTH-uh-sihss) a logical guess about what will happen in an experiment

method (METH-uhd) a way of doing something

observations (ob-zur-VAY-shuhnz) things that are seen or noticed with one's senses

reflect (ri-FLEKT) to bounce or send back light rays, sound, or heat from a surface

solar (SO-lurh) having to do with the sun or powered by the sun's energy

solar collectors (SO-lurh kuh-LEK-turz) devices that collect and concentrate heat energy from the sun and turn it into useful forms of energy

FOR MORE INFORMATION

BOOKS

Color Me Science. New York: Children's Press, 2008.

Landau, Elaine. *The Sun.* New York: Children's Press, 2008.

Walker, Niki. *Harnessing Power from the Sun.* New York: Crabtree Publishing Company, 2007.

WEB SITES

Energy Information Administration—Energy Kid's Page: Solar Energy

www.eia.doe.gov/kids/energyfacts/sources/renewable/solar.html#fromthesun

For more information about solar energy and its uses

PBS Kids—ZOOMsci: Solar Cookers

pbskids.org/zoom/activities/sci/solarcookers.html

Find instructions for making another type of solar cooker

U.S. Department of Energy—Roofus' Solar & Efficient Home

www1.eere.energy.gov/kids/roofus/

Click on parts of a virtual home to find out how it uses solar energy

INDEX

absorption, 9, 10–11, 12, 15, 25, 28
absorption experiments, 8–11, 12–15, 25–28
air, 11, 20

carbon dioxide, 24
clean water experiment, 17–20
colors, 9, 10–11, 12, 15, 16, 25, 29
colors experiments, 8–11, 12–15
conclusions, 6, 10–11, 15, 20, 23–24, 28, 29
condensation, 20
condensation experiment, 17–20
cooking experiments, 25–28, 29

do-it-yourself experiment, 29

electricity, 28
evaporation, 17, 18, 20
evaporation experiment, 17–20

heat, 5, 8–9, 11, 12, 15, 17, 20, 25, 28, 29
heat experiments, 8–11, 12–15, 25–28, 29
hypotheses, 6, 9, 12, 18, 22, 25, 29

light, 5, 8–9, 10–11, 12, 15, 16, 21–22, 24
light experiment, 21–24
light waves, 16

notes, 5

observations, 5, 6, 8, 19, 29

photosynthesis, 24
plants, 5, 21–22, 24
plants experiment, 21–24

questions, 5, 6, 9, 21, 29

rainbows, 16

scientific method, 6–7
scientists, 4, 5, 6
solar cells, 28
solar collectors, 28
sunflowers, 24

water cycle, 20

About the Author →

Christine Taylor-Butler is a freelance author with degrees in both civil engineering and art and design from MIT. When Christine is not writing, she is reading, drawing, or looking for unusual new science ideas to try. She is the author of more than 40 fiction and nonfiction books for children.